STECK-VAUGHN
NEW WAY
HEADS and TAILS

Jip!

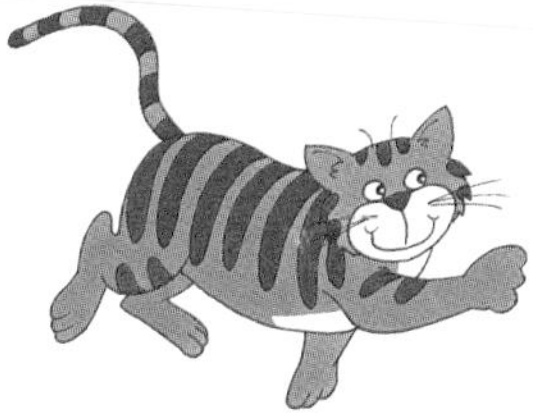

D1519660

STECK-VAUGHN®
COMPANY
A Division of Harcourt Brace & Company

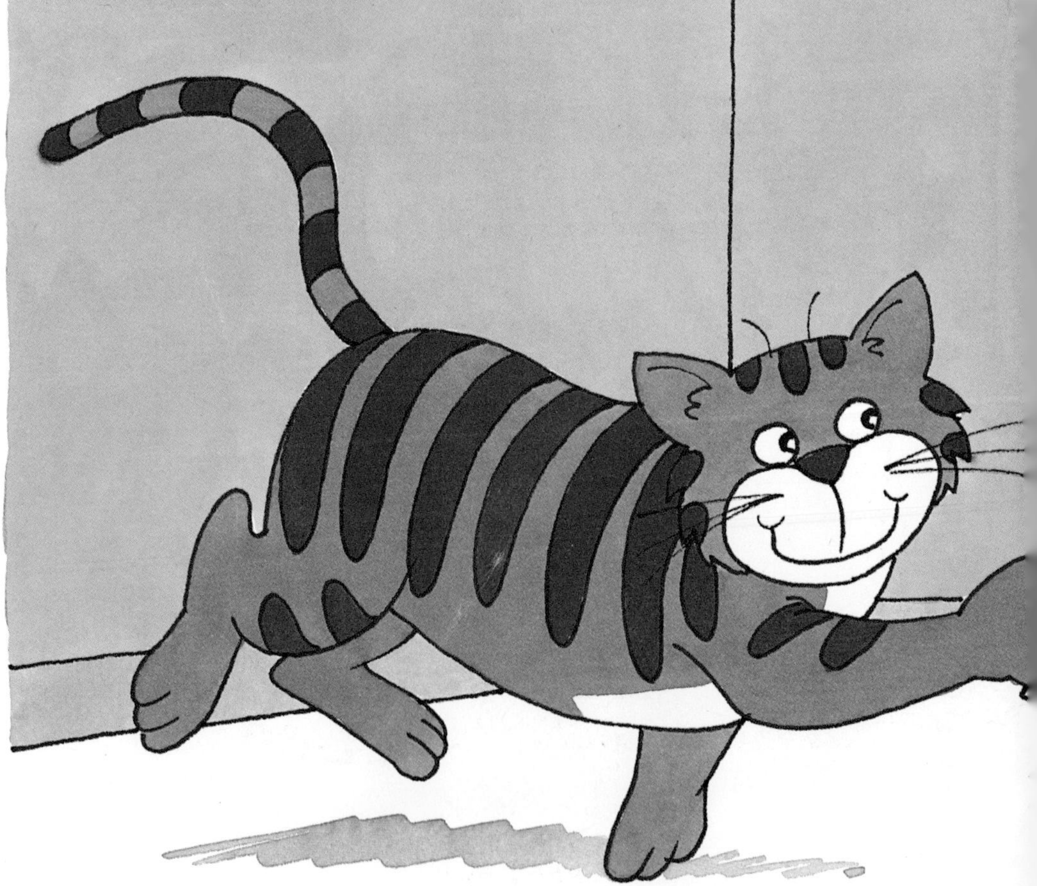

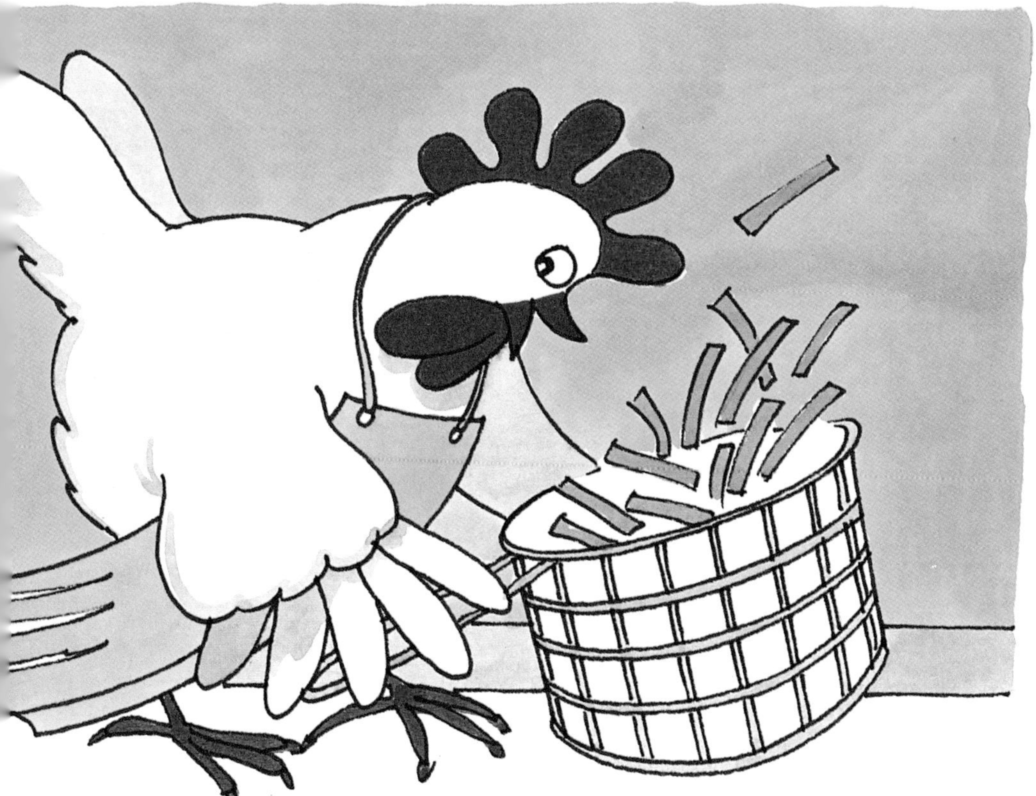

a rip

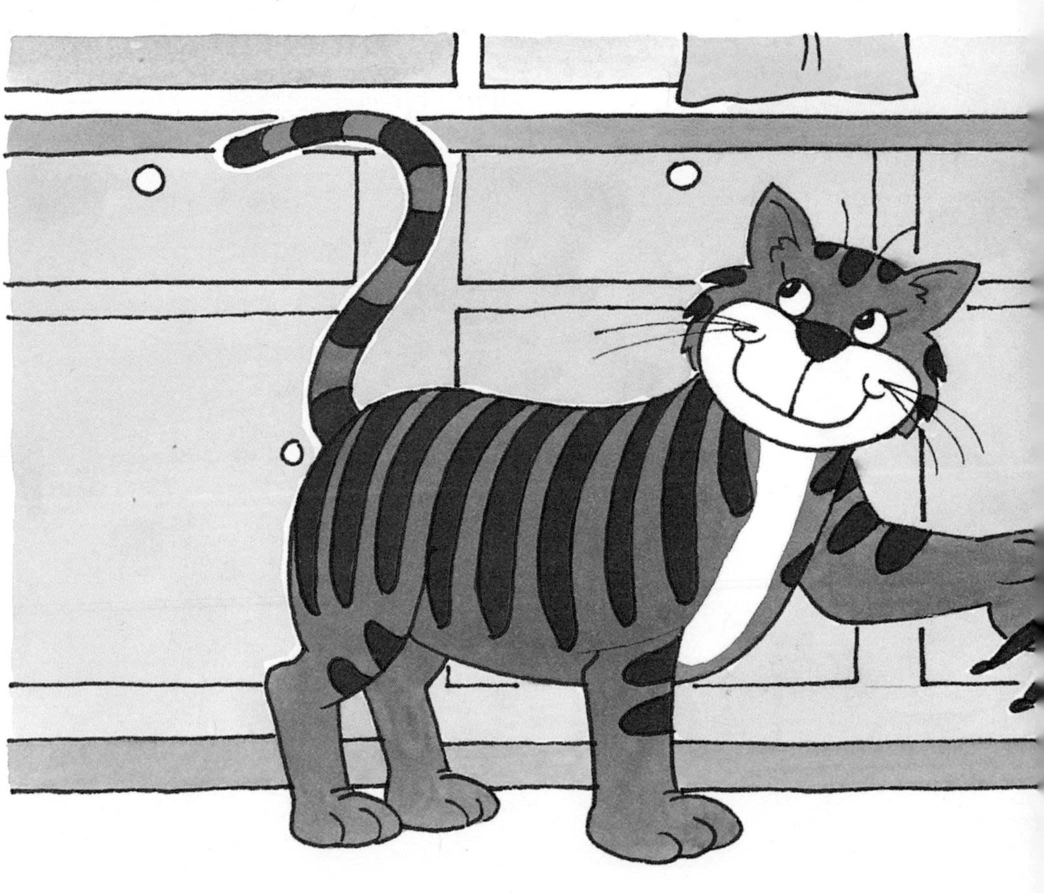

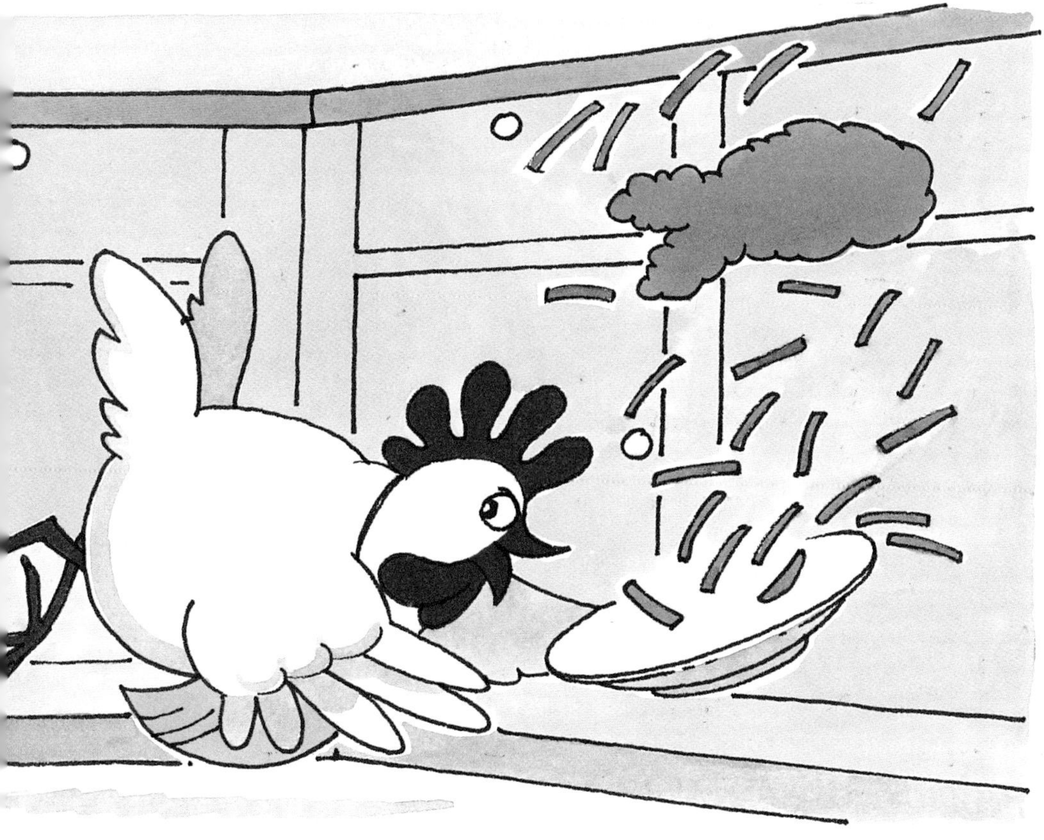

a trip

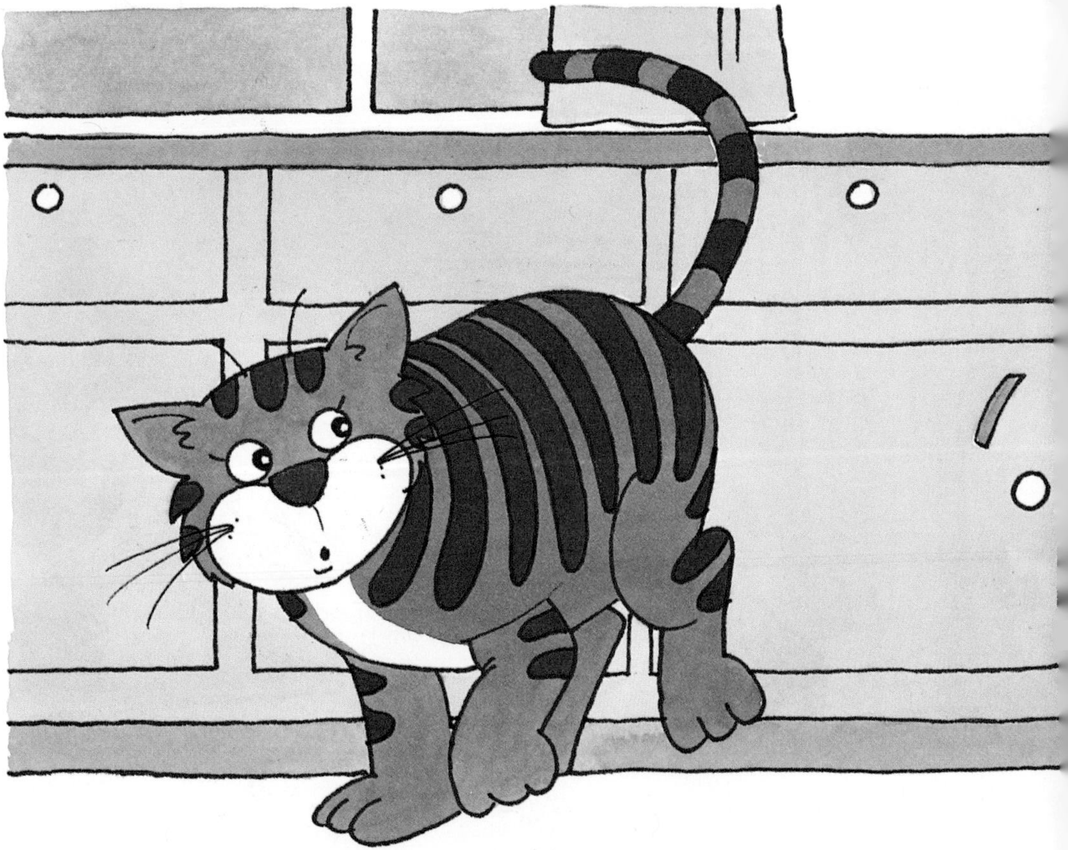

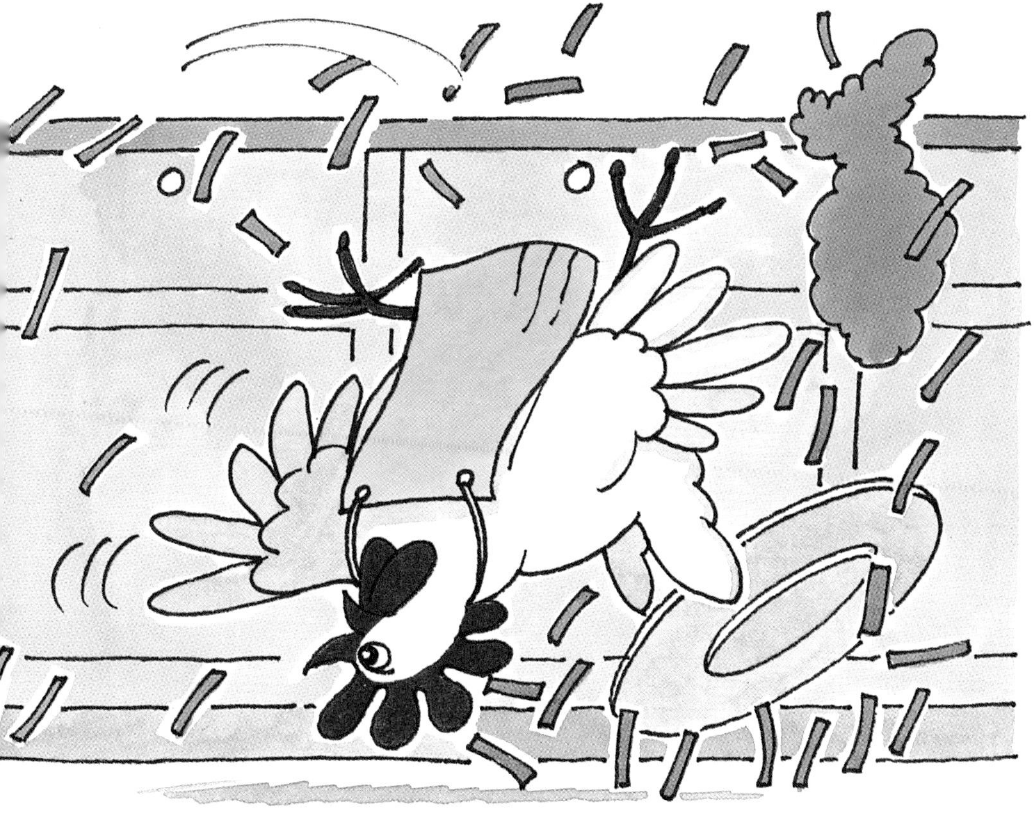

a flip

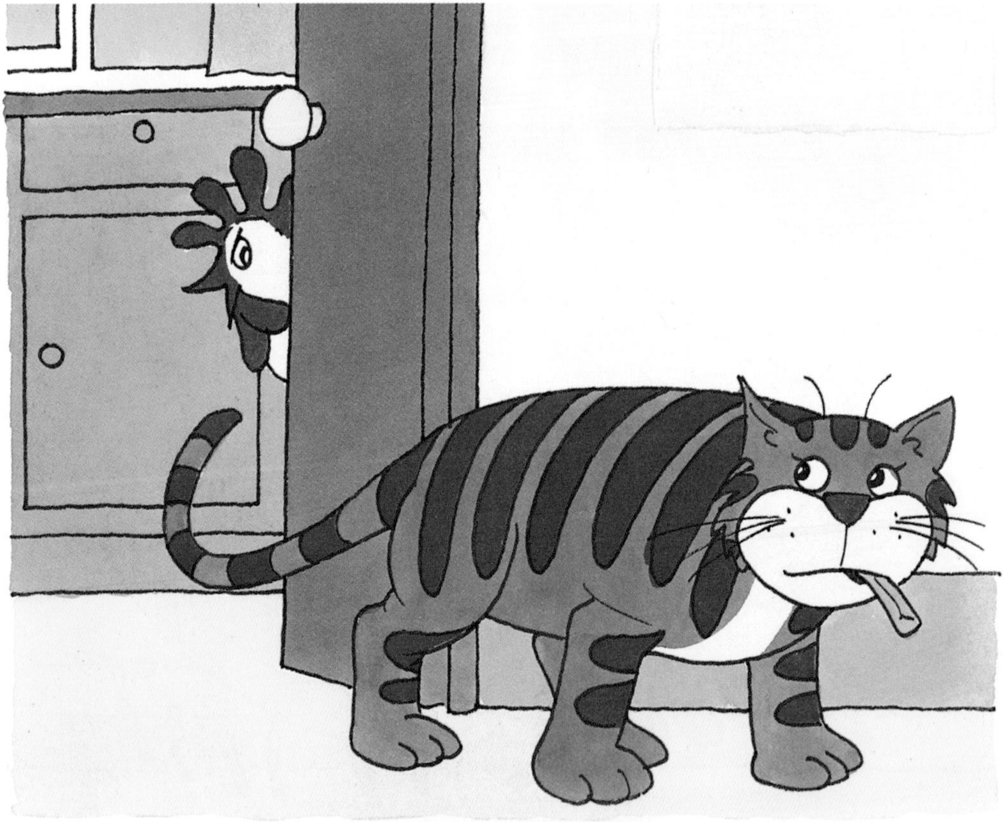

Jip!